WENT LIKE IT CAME

GEOFFREY O'BRIEN

DOS MADRES

2023

DOS MADRES PRESS INC.
P.O. Box 294, Loveland, Ohio 45140
www.dosmadres.com   editor@dosmadres.com

Dos Madres is dedicated to the belief that the small press is essential
to the vitality of contemporary literature as a carrier of the new voice,
as well as the older, sometimes forgotten voices of the past. And in an
ever more virtual world, to the creation of fine books pleasing to the
eye and hand.

Dos Madres is named in honor of Vera Murphy and Libbie Hughes,
the "Dos Madres" whose contributions have made this press possible.

Dos Madres Press, Inc. is an Ohio Not For Profit Corporation and a
501 (c) (3) qualified public charity. Contributions are tax deductible.

Executive Editor: Robert J. Murphy

Illustration & Book Design: Elizabeth H. Murphy
www.illusionstudios.net

Typeset in Adobe Garamond Pro & Avenir Next
ISBN: 978-1-953252-87-6
Library of Congress Control Number: 2023940988

First Edition

ACKNOWLEDGEMENTS

Some of these poems appeared originally in *Bowery Gothic* and *Stride* (UK). "A Story in Memory of John Ashbery" was originally presented in New Delhi in February 2018 at the symposium "Against Storytelling," organized by Amit Chaudhuri; the text was subsequently published by *Fabrique de l'Art* (Kolkata) and *Literary Realism* (New Delhi).

I owe the title of the book, and much else, to Pharoah Sanders (1940-2022).

for Joseph Donahue

TABLE OF CONTENTS

"In a war of rumors and conspiracy theories, identities are stolen and shapeshifting outsiders infiltrate urban parks."

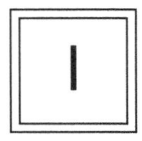

I

A STORY
IN MEMORY
OF JOHN ASHBERY

A Story in Memory of John Ashbery

> All life
> Is as a tale told to one in a dream
> In tones never totally audible
> Or understandable, and one wakes
> Wishing to hear more,
>
> John Ashbery, "Litany"

1

I don't remember where I heard this story.
After the cessation of hostilities
in the Second World War
an American soldier
waiting with so many others to go home
sat cross-legged on the hot deck of a troop ship
reading a paperbound mystery novel—
it might have been *The Camera Clue*
or *The Fatal Kiss* or *The X-Ray Murders*—
and as he came to the end of every second page
he tore that leaf from the book
and passed it to the soldier on his left,
each leaf in turn passed thus
from hand to hand around the deck
until the whole book was read
by hundreds of soldiers with nothing else to do
but measure the time as it leaked away,
so that the cheap little paperback—

it might have been *Reno Rendezvous*
or *Holiday Homicide* or *The Doctor Died at Dusk*—
acquired precious value as one soldier at a time
found a temporary home in some random wad
of narrative padding or incidental description,
some flirty come-on or slangy comeback,
freezing it in place as if by the hypnotic ray
in a comic book, even as the soldier on his left
nudged him to read faster, the way, after all,
the author must have intended, since mysteries are designed
to make time pass as quickly and imperceptibly
as possible, to obliterate time and replace it
with what is experienced as endless and endlessly
pleasurable, even while despite the impulse
to slow down and savor the lovely stillness
of an immobilized sentence the soldier felt driven
to get to the end of it, and if the light held
the last reader on deck would have been left
with a now useless pile of unbound pages,
to be tossed away without thought
just as the details of the story itself—
it might have been *The Fall Guy*
or *Four Frightened Women* or *Weekend with Death*—
were quickly forgotten by each of the soldiers
who had clung to those words as to the side of a life raft
but afterwards didn't even need to make an effort
not to forget what was already being erased,

2

in the diminishing light the elements of the story
popped and went out, it could have been the one
about the missing will or the missing person,
the blackmailed movie star, the body
in the locked room, the wronged convict
looking for payback from the man who sent him up,
the voice rasping threats in the dark after midnight,
the rattling of the bolted storm window,
the redhead with a yen for trombone players,
the tennis pro hiding more than one disgraceful secret,
the Scotch and soda that didn't taste quite right,
what the hat check girl from Club Esquire
whispered to the owner's bullnecked chauffeur,
the fallen hairnet, the half-smoked cigarette,
the galoshes still dry after the rainstorm,
the bent key slipped into the green handbag,
the silk nightgown tossed in the hamper
the way no woman ever would,
but the killer didn't know that—

3

and by then the exhausted soldier has dropped
into a place where not even a Scotch and soda
could help him keep the tell-tale trace
from melting in his hands
while the mind struggles to reassemble
a story with the same name but a different plot—
and by now even the name has changed,
maybe it has become *Ghost of the Shower Handle*
or *Green Horses* or *The Tangled Beans*—
but it hits a skid from the get-go, spins out
into a different century with freakish weather,
where a body with anomalous biological traits
inhabits a zone of methane baths,
in swift eely leaps transmuting the story of anybody
to the story of nobody or more strictly no body,
the dream becoming a commemorative album
on the death of the dreamer
just as he crashes into the brittle wall of light

4

coughing and flicking shards away
and wondering whether dreams
are failed attempts at storytelling,
what with their all too familiar technique
of digression within digression
yanking always further from a main thread
not to be found again, lost
beyond naming, or on the other hand
are stories inadequate attempts
to approximate the dream experience,
imposing a wide-awake logic that will always
remain alien to what it most wanted to capture?
The dreams of the dead have left no trace
but how their stories have piled up, stories of legacies
and massacres and rudely interrupted house calls,
it might have been *The Tale of the Mistaken Twins*
or *The Chastised Wife* or *The Fate of the Orphan*,
judges compiling death sentences for a secret court,
rustled cattle, talking fish, luminescent blossoms,
nothing finally but ordinances and omens,
vows and curses, challenges and predictions,
messages carried by wind across water
to the far shore where they are broadcast like thunder,
louder than any sound in any dream—

5

the dream in a story about a dream
being more elegant than any ever actually dreamt,
the twin dreams for example in the *Arabian Nights* tale
of the impoverished Bagdad merchant
to whom in sleep a messenger appeared
saying "go to Cairo to find a great treasure"
and who arriving without resources
fell asleep in a mosque where a robbery took place
and being mistaken for a robber was beaten and abused
until the police chief asked him why he came to Cairo
and he related his dream and the police chief uproariously amused
by the gullibility of anyone who would put faith in a dream
told him how he once had more or less the same dream
instructing him urgently to go to Bagdad
to a house described in meticulous detail which the merchant
silently recognized as being none other than his own
and on returning to his homeland obeyed the instruction
to excavate the fountain at the end of the garden
thereby uncovering the predicted treasure,
no story could be neater, its crisscross pattern
even cancels itself out leaving no mess behind
as if it were literally the story to end all stories,
as if finally there had been enough stories—
except that this evidently cannot be the case
since when that moment threatens to arrive

it only generates a further story,
a story about precisely the end of all stories
and that turns out to be merely the overture
to the multivolume saga *The End of All Things*
that will generate spinoffs and prequels
and heavily promoted follow-ups
of which *Part Twelve: Beyond Nothing*
will serve as teaser for *My End Is My Beginning*—

6

This had been going on longer
than anyone was in a position to remember,
there was not even a name for the tribe of humans
who over a period of seventeen thousand years
had inhabited continuously a cave
fifty feet wide and five hundred feet long
yet you might be permitted to imagine
that in all that time nobody dropped the ball
as they practiced in the dark rearranging plot points
deleting kinks and dead spots along the way
like a story conference lasting millennia

7

and when having emerged to the light
they invented theater
the principals went into their dance
dressed up as lovers who hyperbolize and are forgiven
as lovers who are not forgiven and are slaughtered
as lecherous servants who always
in some sideways fashion speak truth
skinflints who rage and are mocked
bandits who triumph through disguise
brothel keepers who smuggle messages
clowns who stagger through alleyways
knocking over buckets and fruit stands
householders who tremble for fear of thieves
girls too beautiful to be hidden
warriors turned monstrous from lust
crones who explicate lost bloodlines
a procession of stick figures
and their living shadows
each both itself and
the opposite of the other
unsolvable mixtures
ghosts who sing
animals who prophesy
chasms that open in the ground
to show where the wealth was hidden
long before the story began
just so there would be something or other to restore—

8

millennia of disconnected anecdotes
like my uncle told about a drunken brawl
at Coney Island or a three-day blizzard
or a school chum dying of sepsis
from a dirty jackknife, figments of a gone world
for which the story is no substitute—
the story is nothing
or not more than the length of thick celluloid
by which a professional burglar pries his way
into the closet where the stash is, not more
than the weather they moved around in
all the while they were telling it,
not more than what hangs on it,
props, perfumes, backtalk, smoke,
the crinkling sound from the adjacent room
reachable by no other method
and not even then—

9

as the child found who, trying to decide
which Classic Comic to read when he had read them all,
hoping to find one that would still—
still and always—seem new even after
it was more familiar than his hand turning the pages—
it might have been *Lorna Doone* or *The Talisman*
or *Tom Brown's School Days*—told himself
"I want a story that is not like a trap"—
as he started to fear that every story is a trap
that lures past the greenery of the entryway
into aisles ever narrowing,
whether of barracks or churchyard or schoolroom,
without hope of a reverse maneuver—
and so went poking along the seams of the stories
for the empty space,
the green and dripping glistening light
of the place where the story stands still—
Deerslayer's Glimmerglass or the endless Siberia
of Michael Strogoff—the zone of unending interlude
where the travelers have lunch and savor guitar music
and because the story has stopped
they never in the end resume their journey
and consequently are spared
the drought-ridden badlands
plagues slag heaps corrupt marauders

tax collectors torturers slavedrivers
blighted orphanages airless chapels
the confusions and betrayals
waiting for all who manage to reach the city—

10

I don't remember where I heard that story
and certainly it has changed beyond recognition
I remember hearing about a person
who sat down once a year
to write down the details of the particularly
disturbing incident that had haunted a lifetime
choosing to write them down without ever consulting
the earlier drafts and at the end of many decades
laid them side by side to find
a suite of unrecognizably different stories,
nothing remaining but arbitrary narratives
so blatantly concocted as to be beyond belief
yet no less true since there they are,
they never go away—
by their very survival
they confirm there are no untrue stories,
there is nothing *but* truth,
it occupies every point of space,
seals the exits, the wallpaper is made of it,
the accumulation of foxed and partly shredded
childhood storybooks is made of it, the orange sun
going down out on the street is made of it,
even for the bystander perched outside it
the outsideness is made of it, what doesn't
fit into it is tangled in its main works,

11

while meanwhile—back at the ranch
as my uncle would have said—
even as the story was being ironed out
the thing that actually happened went off
on its own tangent, it did happen,
it did, there *was* a sun in the street
but once only, such being the monstrous condition
imposed on the living who find relief only
in the story that can be taken as needed
even though each telling alters it,
yet after all the freedom to alter it
is what makes it a story, it wouldn't
amount to much without the malleability
that comes close to the heart of ecstatic delight,
while the event—the jackknife
or the brutal happening at Coney Island—
stays locked up in its truth, warehouse beyond access,
it would not be truth if it were not inaccessible,
if they could touch it they would change it,
they do change it and it is no more,
and spend the remainder of their time
wondering where it went, that incident
which was purity itself and since purity
is beyond them it bedevils them
until they make or stumble upon

a story to be a stand-in
like a puppet or a candle
a splash of indigo
a stain a mere splinter
a signal going off in the air
a signal going off the air—

12

you want to hear it
you're afraid to hear it
you're tired of hearing it
you tell it to yourself
you imagine others telling it to themselves
you want to hear it again over and over
you've never heard it
it has been deliberately kept from you
you would pay to hear it
you wish you hadn't heard it
you would pay to forget it
you heard it but you can't remember it
no one ever heard it
it has never been told
it tells itself
it will be telling itself with no one left to hear

CAVE YEARS

Wanderers

With footfalls
on rock flake and feather glue
on crushed grass and reed slime
we make our way out of the lake world

A reversed landscape
to which we woke in the dark
all signals lost
feeling for the path to the mooring cove

So connected we are
that even while alive
we already imagine
we have come back from the dead

The Bed

There are moments
when the sun is nothing

orange glow
staining a blank wall

and the dying see doorways
not visible to others

but cannot enter them
or even stir from the bed

where they beat their hands
against the barrier

A Play

What was a play?

A thunder shower in a garden
A brandy glass knocked off a table

The gowned woman emerging from the hall
A barbed retort from the sofa

The lull while the sky darkens
And a couple whisper fiercely in the half-light

The offstage music as the guests file back
The argument by the doorway

The colors altering and gliding
The long stride toward the window

The recital of a terrible memory
The characters fading into the blackout

To return eternally as actors

Biographical Note

Her childhood among circus performers
Her lessons
From an itinerant engraver
Politics from the air
Discerning in a pamphlet by Marx
Traces
Of the inhabitants of a coral reef
Everyone was her family
Even the damaged part-time poet
With his rage and his theory
Of the ellipse as wavering gateway
Prophet of love and of a peril
As unanticipated as the misstep
Of an uncle on the high wire
"Art is made in the space between mistakes"

The Recluse

Whatever can be uttered
can be corrupted

so he found a new way to write a poem
by only setting down words not part of it

leaving just enough space
to permit glimpses through the gaps

of the true poem and how different it was
from what largely concealed it

bare and disentangled
liberated even from being visible

The Revenants

You have seen the faces and can still hear the voices
In the dark the bodies appear to possess their own evasive will
You direct them to climb a flight of stairs and turn left when
    they reach the top
But they retreat to where they have not already been
In silence you shadow them along their path
You lose them at the bend of the corridor where each turns
    into another
They answer each other's whispers
You intercept a broken piece of giggle or groan
They go on inventing their own stories about what they
    pretend is happening
The voices level out into incomprehensible murmur
They continue ahead without asking
They brush away the overhanging clumps of darkness that
    block their path
Exposing here a wobbly ledge
And there an opening that closes when the light hits it
There is a residual stirring where they pass
A disturbance not quite settled

Distances

I have seen the distance
        from a petal in a vase
to the top of the table
        it rested on
spread out as vast
        as the steppes
and even seen
        the gap between
where other spaces
        leaked in
black distances
        from elsewhere
a blink
        within a blink

Advance Screening

The last person
I expected to see there
Was him

Looking back at me from his front row seat
His eyes bright with astonishment
At the foreign movie
Neither of us had even heard of

And indeed
He was not there

The Authorship Question

How could you be expected
to know if you had written this
the day you came upon it on the closet shelf
where it had been tucked away
too many years ago for any previous tenant
to be consulted about the provenance
of this yellowed typescript,
the words of a stranger
made doubly strange
by the way that in the wavering
of your partial recognition
the double strangeness could only be redoubled?

Preface to a Lost Collection

Lady of lights and shadows
whose poetry designs or perhaps merely deigns

to hide within the conventions
of a devotional verse scarcely distinguishable

from the liturgy it so clearly aspires
simply to utter as if by rote

one further time
and at each repeat

transact anew
a bond with what stays changeless

(rose, blood, sun, tongue,
eye, hand, wellspring)

with only the tiniest variance
to refresh the template

deliberately left empty
save for what fills it out

through all the veins and halls
to the limit of its unimaginable brim

Goodbye to My Books

I dream of books
The most recent was a history of doorknobs

It began in some way with Stendhal
A suite of interiors under perpetual surveillance
A laptop ripped off hours later from a motel room
What was on it
How did they get in

This has been going on from the start
The books take many forms
They constantly approach formlessness without ever
    managing to get there

There was the book that consisted of a wide channel of water
There was the friend whose memoirs turned out to be the
    story of my life
Viewed from an angle at which that story was folded into
    an elongated reflection
A wordless glimmering streak

I walked like a ghost among his sentences

Fell in love with people who made wide detours
Around the murky columns of a drowned city
And were not seen again

There had never been a chance to talk
Or learn anybody's name

It seems they are alive and doing well there

The city held yet more books
Warehouses full of them lined the wharves
Inside there were always others
To be hauled up from the damp archive

Catalogues of airplane parts
Half-rotted telephone directories
Metal-bound magical grimoires

Dialogues with a luna moth
Scrupulously footnoted

A scroll poem
That mutated into an overhead view of a flowery plain
Across which an armored horde galloped
The letters themselves being the ruts their chariots made

Some of the books acquired worldwide celebrity
Such as Patrick Britten's diptych *Paris meurt* and *Paris ne
    meurt pas*
A work said to have "invented language for a second time"

The books elude contact
Can be too slippery to handle

Sentences murmur
As they collapse inward

The words are tiny people
Who barter objects in what seems like a marketplace
They yell at each other or exchange blows

Nothing written down in a book
Is allowed to stand still
Long enough to seize hold of

The eyes blur
The paper is too far away
As the letters become progressively smaller
I try to become small enough
To follow them into the book

The book dissolves in the dark
Like the gems in ancient stories
That turn into waterdrops

Some of these books I wrote
Although I can no longer remember what is in them

PLAGUE YEARS

Welcome to Semblance

The calm and well-ordered traffic patterns of Semblance
belie its vibrant industrial capacity

Even the houses with their toylike elegance
link up to remote sources of energy
that without appropriate maintenance
portend havoc

Semblance has parks, plazas, and a depot
constructed not long after the invention of steam

Distinguished individuals born or long resident in Semblance
include a band leader, an instructor of physical exercise,
several government appointees, and the founder of a food chain

It is perhaps best known for its cloudless afternoons

Vicissitude

This new emperor
is not so bad

This new emperor
is a fucking nightmare

This new emperor
seems kind of great

but wait a minute
the soldiers just killed him

This new emperor
comes from some place

I never heard of
way up north

Song in Winter

What is their thought?

To catch the uncaught,
to buy the unbought,

to detect and collect,
to restrain and contain,

to exclude the precluded
and delude the included,

to name, to defame,
and after to maim,

to blare, to blur,
to scare, to slur,

to vent the invented
and subtract the fact,

to gather, to tether
in bundles together,

to hold and hoard
and live as lord.

After Q Who

After Q goes silent, something else must come,
R perhaps, but of what might R be prophet?
Red revolution in the wake of riotous rebellion,
rabid revulsion triggering reckless realignment,
rowdiness reveling in retaliatory roughhousing?
In the reeking residue of reactionary repression
rancid regression roils raucous ruckus.
Radical redefinition racks up right-minded rulings,
and radiant rejoicing reaps rude revilement.
Any remote reverie of rapt reflectiveness,
rhapsodic revelation or rapturous reawakening,
reckons without the relentless rigmarole
of rote redeployment and resigned reeducation.
Ruined roadways are repositories of rubble,
rackets run rodeos of rapacity.
Rather as recluse relish reflexively rock rattle and reef rim,
and in rune a remnant of reed rustle and rain.

August 2020

Sounds never heard.
Silences never heard.
Signs never seen.

Words known
and sounded in the head
but never before out loud.

Faces never recognized
even two feet away
that now are without mask.

Criminals of the Galaxy

Hard to find a door when you no longer can say
what a door is, harder even to retrace the steps
not yet taken, especially when the alarm system
turns out to be sensitive to movement merely imagined,
hair trigger doesn't half say it, and they don't
take birthdates for an answer, will deny even that the names
were accurately registered, "stage managed" is one way
to describe the effect when striplighting clicks on
and the boarding portal with its marks of forced entry
is seen to have been replaced by a blatant simulacrum,
proof if such were needed that they don't and have never
cared much about nuance, are in fact not capable,
it is only then that what has been called "getting it"
kicks in just late enough to make the whole enterprise
the pilot for a seemingly unmarketable mind game,
pitifully under-conceptualized, if not for the trace elements
of someone else's blood in the surrounding air.

Acetone

"colorless, highly volatile and flammable,
with a characteristic pungent odor"

"I come now once more to a place where the temptation to hesitate,
or to hint rather than state, is very strong" (Lovecraft)

This is the history of a drowning out
by low-vibration impulses from beyond or beneath us
in a time when the sky is no longer the sky
but rather something like an immense mirror,
its blue a prismatic trick to disguise
the fact of removal in the impending era
of polar darkness and pale horizons.
This is a history of metallic lull,
of silence prickly with remote interferences,
of phrases hardwired to signify the reverse
of their commonly misunderstood meaning;
the history of substitution; of twinning
and undetected merging; of windows repurposed
to conceal what they look out on.
Merely to make one entity resemble another
is an ancient game for the reptilian intellects
to whom we are tokens moved around the board.
I am speaking of the ones who have cracked open our heads
and feed now as they please.
Before forms were they were.

Their faces hide behind their faces.

When you stop looking they turn into themselves.

By now your neighbor might be someone else

or not anything at all, a digitized blueprint

given the illusion of life and breath

by a species of electricity generated elsewhere

for ends unknowable to any but those

who will take our place or have already begun to

at scattered points throughout the city,

gas stations and barber shops,

clinics and supermarkets,

which are no more than vents or delivery chutes

that if mapped would show a pattern, an encrypted manual

for a universe invented behind your back.

Years of infiltration modified a township

into a rip in the fabric of space

through which aliens scurry like nocturnal rabbits,

the park into a maze of hypnotic maneuvers

where depth has no bottom

and the thread no end,

and the moon over the garage into a hollowed-out heliport.

Sidewalk

If I had nothing
If I had nothing

Against the wall
Or down the street

Against the sun
Or against time

If I had nothing
To say to anyone

Who had not
Already gone

I would be interrupted
I would fade

Into the cool air
Of April night

SOLSTICE SOLO

Solstice Solo

As if voices
had no bodies

Or names
no beings attached to them

Or beings no names
or none quite part of what contains them

Snapshots that melt on being seen
documents dissolved by the act of reading

Remnant crumb scoured away
as syllables are scoured
by creek stones

The indecipherable chatter
of unseen children
registering as fountain water
or patches of glare

Foreclosed grotto
where names go
to find out where they were born

Disembodied greeting
cork croak
oracle babble

Crank of links
prong of rungs
ring of pangs

A tone thin
as silver foil
if its glint
were audible

Different towns
calling for different names
and names needing lives
to back them up

They wore masks
out of kindness

After a few hours
they forgot who they had been
and by the time they remembered
the doorway was already off limits

The secret starer
in love with darkness

Ghost woman
rifling the doctor's desk
after the war

The message
intended to undermine everything
written in a disguised hand

After she came back
she was not the same person
it was even a question
whether she had been there before

A past no more substantial
than a bit of torn rag
or some grains of rice
adhering to a burnt cookpot

What effort to sustain
over seven decades
a lineage of momentary certainties

Amid gathering haze
or distracting ambient sibilance
we inhabit our distance from where we are
from all that was once close enough
to mistake for an extension of ourselves

Try as you will
you cannot impress the dead
who are compounded of different minerals
and under the ancient sun
continue to scratch marks where none will read them
of blinded king and fallen tower

While in a successor state
to which none are native
feral pigs
and gluttonous toxic weeds
feed on ragtag air under a gray rim

Theory of a world
drained of color and liquid
deprived of texture
and unmoored from pleasure
theory of a dead world

Not yet lost
and already unredeemable

A signal can go silent
for a thousand years
can go silent until the art
of detecting signals
is lost forever

They will walk around
knowing nothing
of what was never heard

Bewildered in a maze
of frequencies no longer apprehended

All I know is
it was there
the last time I looked

The sirens sang
the absence of any ocean

Dry river
left rock forms
as skeleton

The branches sway
in the dusk light
as if they had never
encountered wind before

How trees feel
when wind knocks them
or rocks when icebound
is not to be compared
to the anger of animals

Least of all the humans
who love to think
they invent their world
instant by instant

What do you imagine the others were doing
for the last five hundred thousand years

They had all the time in the world
to make everything up
to corroborate the enmeshments
of what never happened

Mapping the sea
as if it were a passive onlooker
a decorative backdrop to the dramas of land
to fill out the empty spaces
where humans and their languages are not

What they might be
without their languages
without their poems
still not resolved

Out of fathers sisters
mothers and brothers
out of their living bodies
having received words

The words
were people once

We are tangled
in their echo

Caught up
the way root clings to soil
or soil to rock
until wrenched

Nothing can be hidden
anything can be lost

News comes
of ripples sent out
through the fabric of space

The nightmare of time
stubbornly refusing to pass

In a living room
where conditions erode
moment by moment
as if it were a continent
over the course of a millennium

Tired of keeping watch
the houses shift their gaze

I swim underneath time
as under thick ice

Startled to wake
in a body that resembles shale

Without connection
altogether separated out
a motet whose notes are stone

To see
as through a lens
what it was like to be constructed
piece by piece
like an apartment building

An achieved form
seeking nothing beyond itself
neat as a button
at the bottom of a drawer

A button come loose
no longer tied to anything

An object that a child might study
who finds shrines on shelves
and oases in attics

At the age
when a piece of music
is known like the body of a phantom lover
caressed by its changes
without being touched

Music
the only possible
description of silence

A pause the hardest work

Chirps in fog
after rain
a piano fragment

Silhouette
of an imperceptible presence
traced from what was lying around

Items tucked away in dwellings
separated by hundreds of miles
forming a pattern
knowable only to the dead

Counters for a local economy
of no value beyond the surrounding hills
yet heavy within the zone
with the freight of bristly surfaces
and garden smells

God wind laden
with perfumes and bitters

Once there were gods
in the garden
now not even a garden

In the chronicles
the spirit is encountered
speaks through branches
rustled by wind gust

and being recognized
dissipates in mist

First was light
then eyes
that took almost forever to open

Is the border paused
is the border frozen
are the boats
motionless in the channel

The photorealism of dreams
unmatched by any camera
delineates the musculature
even of what is not here

Closely observed flight patterns
of tiny birds never seen on earth

A space cleared
in the absence
of what passed for life
that swarms now
with reawakened silence

Tensely alert as if migrating

ABOUT THE AUTHOR

GEOFFREY O'BRIEN, born in New York City in 1948, has published nine collections of poetry, among them *Floating City* (1995), *Red Sky Café* (2005), *Early Autumn* (2010), *The Blue Hill* (2018), and most recently *Who Goes There* (2020). He is also the author of prose works including *Hardboiled America* (1981), *Dream Time: Chapters from the Sixties* (1988), *The Phantom Empire* (1993), *The Browser's Ecstasy* (2000), *Sonata for Jukebox* (2004), *Where Did Poetry Come From* (2020), and *Arabian Nights of 1934* (2023). His writings on film, music, theater, and poetry have appeared frequently in *The New York Review of Books* and other periodicals. He worked as editor at Library of America for 25 years, retiring as editor in chief in 2017. He lives in Brooklyn.

Other books by Geoffrey O'Brien
published by Dos Madres Press

Who Goes There - 2020

For the full Dos Madres Press catalog:
www.dosmadres.com